Multiethnic Church

A Case Study of an Anglican Diocese

Delbert Sandiford

Formerly Executive Officer,
Minority Ethnic Anglican Concerns, Diocese of Southwark

GROVE BOOKS LIMITED
RIDLEY HALL RD CAMBRIDGE CB3 9HU

Contents

First Impression June 2010
ISSN 0144-171X
ISBN 978 1 85174 760 3

Introduction

Black and minority ethnic (BME) members represent an increasing presence in Christian churches. The English church attendance survey of 2005[1] found that they accounted for 17% of all Christian denominations.[2] This is approximately twice their level of representation in the general population in the 2001 national census.

Whereas white church membership is in decline BME membership is growing, although not sufficiently to offset overall decline. Between the church attendance surveys of 1998 and 2005, white membership fell by 19%, while BME membership increased by 19%. The pattern is the same for both evangelical and non-evangelical Christians. The BME presence is therefore a significant one, and it is possible that without it some churches in the large conurbations would have closed. For example, in the London area a number of Anglican, Methodist and URC churches are over 90% BME, and would be unsustainable without the black presence.

However, we do not see similar levels of BME representation among the leadership of mainstream Christian churches. Mainstream churches, like the wider society, have suffered from inertia in accommodating the BME presence throughout their ministries, governance and liturgies. They have recognized that racial discrimination has played a significant part in this, and over the past 25 years have been using their best endeavours to effect positive change. Good intentions expressed in decisions at synodical level have been slow in bearing fruit on the ground at local church level.

Jesus' life and teaching was inclusive of other ethnic groups. The apostle Paul articulated the vision of the body of Christ which fully embraced all ethnic groups. The church at Antioch lived out this multiethnic vision in its composition, leadership and mission. Two thousand years on we still struggle to make the vision real.

This booklet attempts to set out some intentional action taken by one very multiethnic diocese in the Church of England—Southwark—to bring about greater inclusiveness of BME members throughout its structures. The Diocese recognizes that God is calling everyone, regardless of ethnic origin, to give loving service, and that the barriers to achieving this have to be tackled at local level. This work has been bearing fruit, although slowly and not without some frustration.

2

Post-war Immigration and Racial Discrimination

Immigration and the Growing BME Presence

Our story starts with the large scale immigration to Britain from the Caribbean, Africa and Asia during the Second World War and immediately thereafter. In that war many people from the colonies came to Britain to fight for the mother country. Some remained after the war, but 1948 marked the turning point for immigration with the arrival of 492 people from the Caribbean on board the SS Empire Windrush. We do not have precise statistics of how many BME people were in the UK in the 1940s and 1950s but the best estimate is that there were approximately 74,500 BME people living in the country in 1951. By 1966 the number had risen to approximately 595,000.[3] The figure from the 2001 census was 4.6 million, or 8% of the population. The demographic change has been very rapid.

Racial Discrimination

The drive for immigration was to meet labour shortages. The hospitals and transport systems directly recruited people from the colonies and former colonies. Others came to meet the demand for labour in the textile and service industries. In spite of the evident economic wants that were satisfied by immigration, the newcomers met with racial discrimination generally from the indigenous white people. There was discrimination in employment, housing and services; such racial discrimination was perfectly lawful, and had a long history. The black presence in Britain predated the large scale immigration described above. We know from the work of the black general practitioner Dr Harold Moody, who settled in Britain in 1904, that discrimination on the grounds of race was the norm. Moody was a lay minister in the Congregational Church, which later became part of the United Reformed Church, and he regularly preached and campaigned against racial discrimination in society.[4]

The countries of heritage of BME members were former colonies, although now an increasing number of younger members have lived only in Britain. Colonialism was necessarily a relationship of dependence by the colonies on the metropolitan country. Like slavery in the Caribbean and the Americas, that relationship was predicated upon white people being projected as superior, and black and Asian people as inferior. These roots of racial discrimination were reinforced at every turn in literature, the media and economic arrangements. Such attitudes played a part in the way the newcomers from the Caribbean, Africa and Asia were received in their newly adopted country.

Responses to Racial Discrimination

In 1965 the first Act of Parliament outlawing racial discrimination was enacted. This was a culmination of a long campaign to deal with the issue. It was followed by further Acts of Parliament in 1968 and 1976—each filling gaps exposed by previous legislation. This is not the place to explore how Britain dealt with the phenomenon of racial discrimination in employment, goods, facilities and services, but to register that racial discrimination in the church was part of a larger social problem. Some BME migrants had been members of the Christian faith in their home countries; on arriving in Britain they sought out their local church to worship. Indeed, some arrived with letters of introduction from ministers in their home countries to the local pastor in Britain. But the mainstream denominations—Church of England, Roman Catholic, Methodist and Congregational churches—found it difficult to accept the newcomers as fellow Christians. There was rejection.[5]

> **Mainstream denominations found it difficult to accept the newcomers as fellow Christians**

The response to rejection was that some people left to join or to form black churches. The spin-off from discrimination in church has been the flourishing growth of black Pentecostalists who today represent 45% of all British Pentecostalists, although not all black Pentecostalists were people who had left the mainstream denominations. Others remained in mainstream churches and faced racial discrimination—some passively, some with a passion for getting rid of it. Just as racial discrimination was challenged in the wider society, leaders emerged to challenge this phenomenon inside the church—both black and white members. Among them were people like Wilfred Wood, a black priest who had been born in Barbados and who later became Bishop of Croydon; David Sheppard, a white priest who later became Bishop of Liverpool; and Ivor Smith-Cameron, an Indian priest who had been Canon Missioner at Southwark Cathedral.

Understanding What Racial Discrimination Is

It is relatively easy to spot direct and indirect discrimination. The test is whether an action has an adverse impact on the subject of discrimination. A marker for direct discrimination is whether a person has been treated less favourably on the grounds of colour or race. For indirect discrimination the marker is whether there are criteria which are capable of being satisfied by ethnic groups by and large, but which systemically lead to less favourable treatment of a particular ethnic group. Institutional racism is rather harder to detect, because it is embedded in the processes and culture of an organization. It is defined in the Stephen Lawrence Inquiry report as 'the collective failure of an organization to provide an appropriate and professional service to people because of their colour, culture or ethnic origin. It can be seen or detected in processes, attitudes and behaviour which amount to discrimination through unwitting prejudice, ignorance, thoughtlessness and racist stereotyping which disadvantage minority ethnic people.'[6] In this scenario no-one means to exclude others on the grounds of race, but ignorance and thoughtlessness become a justification for inaction and benign neglect which lead to exclusion.

Ignorance and thoughtlessness become a justification for inaction and benign neglect

Some church-related examples will serve to illustrate the point. Where black and minority ethnic (BME) people are well represented on the church's electoral roll but not on the church council it is easy to rationalize that such underrepresentation is due to BME members not putting themselves forward. There is no evident barrier. Anyone can stand in elections for the church council, and people cannot be forced to offer themselves for election. Not to challenge these perceptions or to ask why the situation exists allows underrepresentation to continue. It is this atmosphere of neglect which gives rise to the complacency that allows exclusion to flourish, and amounts to institutional racism. No one has acted in bad faith. The institutional mindset has created the barrier.

Similar attitudes can be seen in the perception that BME people prefer to be sidespersons and servers but not to offer themselves for the ordained and accredited ministries. This unwitting stereotyping ends in exclusion. The perception that someone's accent might be a barrier to such ministries, or that members should be overprotected against the possibility of not being recommended for ordination training by a Bishop's Advisory Panel, have the best motives in mind but can result in a denial of opportunity. Institutional racism flourishes in such thoughtless attitudes and behaviours.

The overall impact is that part of the worshipping community is not able to contribute abundantly to the life of the church. They are underrepresented in its ministries, governance and liturgy. Such underrepresentation will persist unless it is challenged by church leaders and from within the congregation.

Ethnic and Cultural Difference in the Early Christian Church

Ethnic Tension in the Early Christian Church

The first Christians were Jews, either resident in Judea or members of the Diaspora. They had a shared history but cultural divisions between them soon became evident. Acts 6 exposes discrimination on cultural lines. The Greek-speaking Jews complained that their widows were being given less daily food rations than the Hebrew widows. No attempt was made to justify the unequal treatment. Church leaders quickly addressed the issue by the appointment of seven deacons whose task was to look after welfare matters. This structural solution appears to have sorted the matter out. We hear no more about discrimination against the Greek widows in the remainder of the Acts, although members of the Hellenist group were subsequently expelled from Jerusalem on what appears to have been theological grounds. The role of the temple as the central point of God's presence was the dividing theological issue.

As the story of the early church unfolds we see Philip, one of the deacons, baptizing the treasurer of Ethiopia, who was clearly a proselyte. This was soon followed by Peter's encounter with Cornelius, the first unambiguously Gentile convert to Christianity. The encounter challenged Peter to wrestle with his racial prejudices. Why did it take Peter three attempts to accept Cornelius? The perception of Gentiles as inferior was deeply rooted in Peter's psyche. To accept Cornelius as an equal went against everything he had been taught. It went against his religion. To the Jewish mind Gentiles were uncircumcised and therefore unclean. Yet God was inviting Peter to put his prejudices aside and cross a racial barrier. He accomplished it with great difficulty.

The Church at Antioch

In Acts 13 we have the clear outlines of a multiethnic church—a church that has embraced ethnic difference. This is evident in the make-up of the leadership of the church in Antioch. There was a multiethnic leadership team which included a leader who is clearly black (Simeon, also known as the black man); Lucius of Cyrene, who has a Latin name and hails from North Africa; Manaen, whose name indicates that he was very probably a Hellenist Jew; Paul and Barnabas, representing the Hebraist group. It was this multiethnic, multicultural group which commissioned Paul and Barnabas to undertake the church's first momentous missionary journey. They took the Christian message to communities of Jews and Gentiles in a number of cities in Cyprus and Asia Minor before returning to their home base at Antioch. At this point the strains of creating a multicultural community became unmistakable. The clash of cultures was deeply divisive, and is laid bare in Acts 15.

Giving Leadership on a Divisive Issue

Should the Gentile Christians be expected to sign up to Jewish cultural practice—in particular, circumcision? Does a member of this new community have to be a good Jew in order to become a Christian? The Council of Jerusalem was an intense consultation whose outcome was clear. Gentile members did not have to be circumcised. For those Gentiles who responded to God's grace, membership of the Christian community only required them to believe in the Lord Jesus, to cease to worship other gods and to lead a moral life (Acts 15.20, 29). This was unambiguous, but we know the debate rumbled on and the tension returned.

The tension in the early multiethnic church was a matter of considerable angst to Paul

The tension in the early multiethnic church was a matter of considerable angst to Paul, who devoted a significant part of his letter to the Galatians to the issue. The Torah had got in the way of church membership and church unity. Hebraist Jews continued to insist on the requirement that Gentile converts to the Christian message should be circumcised. This could be a barrier to membership of a religion that was open to all. It mattered because Christianity was breaking new ground. Judaism was a monoethnic faith peculiar to the Jews. It did not seek to convert or include others. Gentiles could become members if they wished, on condition that they fully signed up to the Torah. Small numbers of people who were attracted to Jewish monotheism became proselytes. Christianity, on the other hand, invited everyone to become members.

Paul's solution was to go back to God's promise to Abraham that he would be the father of many nations. In Galatians, Paul argued that this promise had been fulfilled in Christ. Before Christ the law had been created in order to deal with sin and to regulate the behaviour of the Jews. This had put the Jews in a favourable position and interrupted the relationship between God and the Gentiles. As Alan le Grys argues, the interposition of the law had meant that the Gentiles had been left on their own.[7] Christ's death and resurrection had the effect of removing the barrier created by the Torah. His death made salvation available to everyone. All nations would become beneficiaries of Abraham's blessing. Inequality before God had been abolished. But although we are not aware of a convincing counter-argument, the debate may well have rumbled on.

We see Paul returning to the issue in the Letter to the Ephesians. The nub of his concern is expressed in Ephesians 2.11–22. Gentiles had been alienated from Jews and from God. Paul reiterates that access to God is now open to all freely through Christ, and without any barrier. The traditions and ethnic prejudices which had been a barrier (v 14) separating Jews and Gentiles had fallen away.[8] Ephesians points to a new society in which Jews and Gentiles are no longer strangers but are reconciled with God and with each other, and form a cohesive entity. The Law and the racial barriers which it sustained fall away. In such a society all members have equal rights and responsibilities.

When Paul writes in Romans that the church is the body of Christ and all members of the body are encouraged and expected to contribute their gifts according to the grace they have been given, he makes no distinctions on ethnic grounds (Romans 12.4–18). No ethnic group can claim a monopoly on any office or function. Not to contribute your God-given gifts to the life of the church leaves the church incomplete. There is no distinction between Jew and Gentile in the ministry, governance and witness of the church. This is the standard the church has to aim for. When racism is allowed to flourish—whether direct, indirect or institutional—the church falls short of the standard God requires.[9] A state of discrimination which excludes members creates unused gifts in the body of Christ and undermines the Pauline ideal. The task that falls to its members is to recreate a right relationship with God and with each other by rooting racism out. This requires confronting the source of the dysfunctional behaviour and seeking to bring about a true turning away from actions which disfigure the life of the church.

> The gifts he gave were that some would be apostles, some prophets, some evangelists, some pastors and teachers, to equip the saints for the work of ministry, for building up the body of Christ.
>
> Ephesians 4.11–12

4 Community and Culture Today

Ethnicity in Church Today

The message of the biblical texts cited in the previous chapter is a message of community in Christ. How do we translate this into our context today? Old habits die hard. The history behind low levels of active BME participation has to be taken into account in seeking to bring about a transformation. Clergy have to be in the forefront of such change—giving leadership, encouraging the BME members and creating an ethos where everyone is expected and expects to participate.

This means white members being prepared to share power and responsibility, giving up some power in order to bring others in. This can be problematic. A sense of clubbishness can develop in church. Clubs have their own rules about who is in and who is out. There may be unwritten assumptions about who will do the rotas, who will lead the Sunday School, who will lead the intercessions and so on.[10]

The most obvious manifestation of church operating like a club can be seen at coffee-time following the main Sunday service. In ethnically mixed congregations white people will generally congregate together, and BME people similarly congregate together. They may be catching up on each other's news over the past week, but this prevents any meaningful contact between the ethnic groups—the kind of contacts which allow people gradually to get to know each other better and to create bonds of trust and reciprocity between them. It is ultimately such trust and reciprocity which enables people to collaborate with each other across ethnic boundaries. Without it, people remain in their 'comfort zones' and find it easy to justify why things remain as they are.

In discussions with clergy and parochial church councils about who takes on roles in church I have frequently heard white church members make statements like the following about BME participation:

- Black people have only been coming to church recently. They do not have the knowledge of how the church works, so you would not expect to see them in positions of leadership.

- They do not wish to participate actively.

- They have family commitments which make it difficult for them to participate in church roles.

- They have not proved themselves by undertaking leadership roles which give you confidence to put them forward for the church council.

- They have a different understanding of church from white people.

Comments such as these reveal a lack of appreciation of people's worth and commitment. Church members do not know each other. But there is also a certain amount of circularity in the comments. White people were not born into these roles. They had to start somewhere and build up the experience and confidence. Yet BME people are expected to have all the experience *a priori*. Without this experience they become locked into a *Catch 22* situation. Only better understanding which comes from church members behaving less like a club will break down these mental barriers.

Sidestepping Ethnic Segregation

In a church that is becoming predominantly BME it can be a challenge to retain white members, particularly white working-class members, and retain a sense of community appropriate to the context of the area in which the church ministers. What we have been witnessing in some of our churches is that, as action to include BME members in governance and accredited ministries bears fruit, some white members begin to feel uncomfortable. The positive promotion of equality attracts more BME members, and white members begin to leave for other churches. This is an area that is recognized more by anecdotal evidence than in hard research, but it mirrors what has been happening to some schools where research suggests that white flight has been taking place.[11] Evidence from the studies of multiethnic congregations in the USA indicates that white members leave such congregations, and other white people do not join, when they feel they are losing power and influence.[12]

Our situation in Britain is one where people from many different ethnic groups are thrown together. This in itself can create barriers of ignorance, mutual incomprehension, stereotyping and prejudice. Some other barriers are in our own heads. We may see other people in certain roles, but never ourselves in those roles. There was a time not so long ago when BME people could not see themselves as joining the Metropolitan Police. The Met was saying, 'Come and join us' but BME people for reasons of history held back. Barriers in your head are quite real.

In his book *The Dignity of Difference* Jonathan Sacks reminds us that difference is a good thing.[13] Difference means that I have something that you do not have and wish to have. Similarly, you have something that I do not have and wish to have. Exchange between us allows us to meet unsatisfied needs. It is in our mutual interest to do business.

We need a common currency to enable us to do business

Because we are such a collection of different cultural groups we need a common currency to enable us to do business. We often talk about racial integration as the means by which we can do business. This is *not* assimilation and everyone being the same. Integration is about mutual tolerance and dialogue between different groups which enable us to understand each other better, and to relate better to each other.

What are some of the in-group factors that may be holding some communities back?

Immigrants who came to Britain from the Caribbean, Africa, and India in the 1950s and 1960s often had very definite timeframes. They would work, send remittances back to support their families, save or achieve a professional qualification, then return to their country of origin. Did this short-term view get in the way of BME levels of engagement in the institutions of their adopted country? If there was an intention to return to the country of origin after five years, did this condition their expectations and attitudes towards community involvement, the parent-teachers' association of their children's schools or involvement in church? If you are only here for a season are you going to invest much time in these institutions? In reality few people realized their aspiration to return permanently to the Caribbean at the end of five years. This five year timescale was revised upwards, to 10 years, to when the children grew up, to retirement even. The mindset of a limited sojourn persisted, and might have influenced some BME actions in confronting the causes and effects of racial discrimination. It was expedient to keep one's head down and leave the white people to run the church.

Even if the first-generation immigrants had a short timescale in their heads, their children do not share this. They are happy to visit their parents' countries of origin, but they see themselves as British. Britain is their home, and they expect to be treated as equals. They are as well-educated as their white peers. However, we are not seeing them come through in church ministries in the kind of numbers that would be expected. For example, the majority of BME Anglican priests were born outside Britain.[14] It is a reasonable question to ask whether an intergenerational transfer of attitudes from their parents or their experiences of rejection may be influencing the behaviour of the generation born and brought up here.

The Importance of Culture

There are many different heritages in Britain, and therefore at least as many cultures. BME worshippers who were born outside Britain brought their own cultural background with them. So many national and sub-national groups attempting to relate to each other and to rub along together can create friction. Culture affects how we communicate, how we build trust, how we develop relationships. It shapes our expectations of the other and the stereotypes we construct to guide our actions. We do not start with a common currency for relating. The same words and gestures might have different meanings in different cultural groups. Applying our own terms of reference to these expressions may lead to misunderstanding at least, or conflict at worst. Getting it right starts with a willingness to increase our awareness of our own behaviour and values, and a willingness to learn from encounters with different others such that we modify our behaviour in future encounters. This process enables us to learn from experience, and in doing so to build up a reservoir of cultural intelligence which facilitates integration. In the next chapter we look at how the Diocese of Southwark has been approaching some of these issues.

> **Culture affects how we communicate and shapes our expectations**

5 Grappling With the Reality

The Church of England's Response

The Church of England began to address the issue of how to relate with their BME members in the mid-1980s. The Archbishop of Canterbury at the time, Robert Runcie, set up a commission to look at life in the urban priority areas. The Commission produced its landmark report *Faith in the City* in 1985 and one of its recommendations was that the church should establish a Commission on Black Anglican Concerns so that:

- the issues of racial discrimination and disadvantage would be given a clearer and more sustained emphasis in all that the church says and does;

- greater awareness of these issues would be promoted throughout the church;

- there would be removal of barriers to the effective participation and leadership of black people at all levels of church life, particularly the ordained ministry.[15]

The Church of England took this on board and the Committee on Black Anglican Concerns (CBAC) was established under the chairmanship of Bishop Wilfred Wood and had its first meeting in April 1987. This committee under its current name—Committee for Minority Ethnic Anglican Concerns (CMEAC)—continues to tackle institutional racial discrimination in the Church of England structures. CBAC and its successor CMEAC pursued a vigorous programme encouraging dioceses to pull down the barriers that were excluding BME participation. They led from the centre, but the work of delivering inclusiveness had to be done in the dioceses, in the parishes or local churches. If inclusiveness does not take root in the local church it is very unlikely to happen anywhere else in the hierarchy.

The Anglican Diocese of Southwark as an Example

The experience of the Diocese of Southwark will be drawn on to illustrate what this means at a practical level. Southwark diocese covers most of London south of the River Thames and east Surrey. It contains 302 parishes and has approximately 46,000 members on its churches' electoral rolls. Today, approximately 22% of these members are black and minority ethnic. This represents a growing part of the membership. In 2002 the BME proportion was 18%. These numbers are equally balanced between members of Caribbean origin and those of African origin. There is a small number of people of Asian heritage. These numbers come from surveys in which members of congregations identified their ethnic origin themselves using the 16 predefined categories from the 2001 UK national census. (Migration from Eastern Europe following the enlargement of the European Union has had little impact on churches in the diocese so far. The Roman Catholic Church has been the main beneficiary of this recent source of migrants.)

Southwark diocese changed gear in its race relations work in 2000. It was very much influenced by the MacPherson inquiry into the failure of the Metropolitan Police to conclude a successful investigation into the murder of Stephen Lawrence. MacPherson found that the failure came about because of police attitudes towards black people, concluding that the Metropolitan Police was institutionally racist and had much work to do to change its attitudes so that it could begin to provide an effective service to the whole community.

On reading the report, the Bishop of Southwark, the Rt Rev'd Tom Butler, concluded that most of what MacPherson had said about the Metropolitan Police could be said about the Anglican Diocese of Southwark. He commissioned the then Chair of the Commission for Racial Equality, Sir Herman Ouseley, to chair a three-member panel to examine the parishes, boards and committees of the diocese. The Ouseley report concluded that the diocese was institutionally racist, evident in the significant degree of under representation of BME members on church councils at every level of the church's structures.[16] A telling example was the Diocesan Board of Finance which had a complement of 60 members, none of whom were BME.

The Ouseley report was accepted by Diocesan Synod, who committed the resources to implement its 49 recommendations. The Minority Ethnic Anglican Concerns Committee was set up, chaired by the diocesan bishop, to oversee implementation, and two staff members were appointed to work with church councils, boards, committees and staff in taking the programme forward. The Committee's staff provided the stimulus for the work and created resources to support it, but the hard work of integration had to be done by the parishes, committees, boards and diocesan staff.

Four broad strands of work were identified:

- to remove the barriers to BME participation in the ordained and accredited ministries;

Ordained and Accredited Ministry

In chapter two we have explored some of the barriers to ethnic inclusion from the perspective of white members—complacency, racial stereotyping, the perception that accents could be a problem and overprotectiveness. Clergy are important gatekeepers in discerning who would be appropriate candidates for ordained and accredited ministries. It is instinctive for leaders to think that future leaders will look like themselves. Bishops recommend and appoint people in their own image. The vicar feels that future vicars should look like him or her—white, middle class, with a particular type of life experience. How do you persuade these influential ministers that there are other people who do not fit this mould but have all the gifts and graces required for the role?

BME members may themselves have invisible barriers in their own heads. An absence of BME leaders up front may deprive them of role models in particular ministries and governance. So there could be an issue of how to develop people's confidence to enable them to undertake these roles.

The minister has to be encouraging and proactive when this kind of intervention is required. Southwark diocese sought to address these issues in taking forward the programme. Many ministers responded positively. A minority has ignored the programme, sometimes on the mistaken assumption that BME members did not wish to be singled out for any special treatment, or that inclusiveness would come good in the fullness of time without any direct organizational intervention. Recent material emanating from the USA stresses how critical it is to be intentional about creating a multiethnic church.[17]

The ordained and accredited ministries were identified as critical to the success of the programme. If it were possible to change the ethnic composition of the leadership, this would send a strong and clear message to members in the pews that BME people were welcome to participate fully in church life. The three ministries were the ordained ministry, the Reader ministry, and the Southwark Pastoral Auxiliary ministry. (Southwark Pastoral Auxiliaries are lay men and women who are authorized by the bishop to undertake caring and pastoral work in an unpaid capacity following two years of part-time training for the role.) This was necessarily a long-term approach, as it takes up to seven years to complete the process of discernment for the ordained ministry, undertake training at theological college and serve a three-year curacy before being offered an appointment as an incumbent. So starting this process in 2000 we saw in 2007 the first fruits of this process with 3 BME priests home grown in Southwark diocese being appointed priests-in-charge of parishes. There are others in the pipeline from subsequent years' intakes—some currently serving at different stages of their stipendiary curacy, and a number of others in theological training.

Side by side with this there has been a steady growth in the number of BME non-stipendiary ministers (including ministers in secular employment). They undertake a similar programme of training to stipendiary ministers.

What action did the diocese take which made a difference? Bishop Butler announced quite early on to his clergy that they were the blocks to progress and that he expected change. With such clear commitment from the top, change began to happen in terms of numbers of BME members offering themselves for the ordained and accredited ministries. The diocese also initiated a series of vocations road-shows targeted at churches with significant BME membership to encourage people to consider

Clergy were the blocks to progress

God's call to ministry. Well over 100 of these roadshows have been held since the programme was initiated in 2002, and although it has not been possible to conduct a rigorous review of their effectiveness, regular feedback from host churches indicates that they have had an impact and that clergy support the continuation of the programme.

The road show takes place in the service on a Sunday morning. With the vicar's agreement, a team consisting of ordained minister, Reader, and pastoral auxiliary visit the church to talk about God's call. After the service, when tea or coffee is served, the visiting team is available to talk on a one-to-one basis with members of the congregation who have questions to ask about vocations. Vocational literature is also made available for interested members to take home and read. If there is further interest the member is advised to speak with his or her parish priest, and this could lead to a conversation with the local vocational guidance unit and a meeting with the director of ordinands.

One cannot claim that everyone who presents for exploring vocation was stimulated to do so as a result of a vocations roadshow. It is part of a journey, but it could be critical if a church has done nothing about vocation for a long time. It is helpful in role-modelling vocation for BME people, as a deliberate attempt is made to include some BME ministers on the visiting team. Both BME people and white people have responded positively to the road show. The table that follows is a helpful indicator of the impact of overall diocesan efforts (including the roadshows) to grow BME vocation to the ordained ministry. Comparing the situation in 2008 with 2002 it can be seen that some progress has been made.

Ministry	Dec 2002	Dec 2008
Senior appointments (bishop, archdeacon)	2	1
Vicars, priests-in-charge, and other in charge posts	10	19
Assistant curates (stipendiary)	3	8
Non-stipendiary ministers	7	21
TOTAL	**22**	**49**
University and National Health Service chaplains	1	4

Table 1: BME clergy numbers in Southwark Diocese

Southwark diocese has not yet arrived at where it would wish to be, but is well on the journey to becoming more inclusive. Current programmes need to run a while longer until inclusiveness becomes a part of the way the church does its business. To give an indication of the scale of the task ahead, the number of BME vicars and priests-in-charge would have to rise to approximately 60 in order to reflect the current make-up of congregations. As of December 2008 the number achieved was 19.

Church Governance

In 2002 the Diocese of Southwark undertook a survey of the ethnicity of members on church electoral rolls and in governance. Ninety-four per cent of parishes responded, representing approximately 37,000 members. This gave a picture of the proportion of members by ethnic group on the electoral rolls and in governance. It was possible to identify churches where the level of BME representation on the church councils was substantially lower than their representation on the electoral roll, and to prioritize these churches for intervention to tackle the barriers to BME representation. Not all the churches were ready to tackle this difficult topic, but some did. In discussions with church council members two critical barriers were identified. The relatively recent arrival of BME members in the church was perceived as contributing to a lack of awareness of how church governance works. People coming from a church tradition elsewhere in the world need information to enable them to function effectively in their adopted homeland. For example, where the priest in say, Nigeria, is seen as the dominant force and the church council or vestry rubber stamps his decisions, the collegial style of church leadership in the UK may surprise and disempower some people. There is an information gap that has to be made good in order to facilitate participation.

Because of limited opportunities for contact, white and black members may not know each other. It takes time to develop the trust and reciprocity which underpins the process of nominating and supporting people for office. Some churches were then able to put in place initiatives to enable all members to learn more about each other, such as hosting international social evenings and honouring national days of countries from which members had come, for example Ghanaian or Jamaican Independence Day. Suitable BME members were identified for co-option to the local church council or deanery synod. Some were sent on the course on 'How the Parochial Church Council Works' in order to raise awareness levels. These initiatives fed through into better representation within the structures, even though there is still room for improvement.

Racial and Cultural Awareness

Training in racial and cultural awareness was designed to meet the needs of clergy in their encounter with ethnic and cultural difference. A training-needs analysis indicated a range of needs for information and experience. After consultation with the diocesan bishop, archdeacons, and the director of training the following priorities were agreed for a training course:

- Cross-cultural communications;
- Cross-cultural ministry—baptisms, weddings and funerals;
- Empowering BME people;
- Racism awareness.

These topics formed the basis of a one-day course available to all clergy. Over 300 ministers have attended the course, which is compulsory for all clergy new to the diocese. This has been replicated by other churches and organizations outside the diocese. What the course strongly seeks to do is to help participants reflect on what multicultural living means in a church context. Each of the topics covered could take several hours—particularly cross-cultural communications and racism awareness. So what is intended to be achieved in one day is to give participants some tools which they can use for further self-development and to shape future experience.

The course feedback has been consistently positive. The session on cross-cultural ministry led to the compilation of a booklet on the occasional offices which attracted interest from clergy outside Southwark diocese.[18] Life-changing situations often take people back to their cultural roots, and call for sensitivity in ministry. The Nigerian and Ghanaian communities continue to hold naming ceremonies following the birth of a child. These are important initiation events to which ministers are invited—to bless the baby, bless the food and so on. These are not events observed by white members and could create uncertainty for white clergy.

Marriage may be preceded by specific customary events and rituals, such as payment of a dowry, both families giving their permission to the marriage and other rituals. Particular customs may be associated with death and funerals. The wake, open coffins in church to allow people to pay their last respects to the deceased, the marking of the year's mind, are examples of ancient rituals which predated the arrival of Christianity in the heritage countries of some BME people. Clergy need to know these things in order to deliver an effective ministry. Indeed, getting it right can bring new members to Christ.

Empowering BME Members

The diocese has a Black and Minority Ethnic Forum which identifies the issues minorities would like to see action on. It was founded in 1995 to be a voice for BME members within diocesan structures. It does not have to create a fuss from outside in order to bring about change. Anyone can attend its meetings. The forum hosts a conference every year on a theme of interest to its members. It has been helpful in the creation of a skills database which enabled suitable BME members to be identified for co-option to diocesan boards and committees when they were underrepresented. As representation improved and it was observed that there were BME members on committees but they were not speaking at meetings, the forum was instrumental in sponsoring a series of courses in presentation and communications skills to give BME people a voice at meetings. More recently the forum has been exercised with the growing number of black teenagers and young men who have fallen victims to gun and knife crime in London and engaged a consultant to provide parenting classes to support vulnerable parents at churches where a member of the congregation had been a victim.

> **The Black and Minority Ethnic Forum is a voice for BME members within diocesan structures**

Each of the three episcopal areas of the diocese has a local Minority Ethnic Anglican Concerns Committee which gives a local slant to the work programme. For example, the Kingston Committee has concentrated on issues such as the education of black Caribbean boys, mental health in the black community and awareness of the ongoing legacies of the transatlantic slave trade. The Croydon Committee has focused on parenting of teenagers.

The diocese has considered how it works with BME people in its formal and informal structures. Some ethnic groups wish to worship in their own language. The reasons may include difficulty experienced by some in understanding English. This would be true of older people who have no contact through work or education with the white British community. The minority language is the only way they can effectively participate in the worship. Another reason is the fellowship provided by their community whose members may travel substantial distances to attend the worship.

There are a number of minority-language-based congregations in Southwark diocese—Korean, Tamil, Lugandan and Ghanaian. In neighbouring London diocese language-based congregations also include an Urdu-speaking congregation, Chinese, Filipino and Nigerian chaplaincies. These groups are not independent of the Church of England, but neither are they represented in the synodical structures. At a practical level their members belong to a local parish church through which they participate in church governance and which they normally attend for worship with the English and wider congregation. The primary focus of these groups is worship in the indigenous language of the members.

Language-based groups represent a small part of the BME membership of the church and provide a solution to a transitional problem. They are not seen as leading to racially-segregated churches, although this arrangement, on the face of it, appears to run counter to the integration drive. As English becomes the first language spoken by younger members of the community and the heritage language becomes less familiar, the justification for language-based congregations will disappear.

London is the location of many black Christian churches. Many of these black majority churches do not have their own buildings and rent worship space from the Church of England, Methodists and the URC. Indeed, church sharing is quite common in Southwark diocese. The tenancy is subject to a formal contract which specifies times of worship, and responsibilities. The spectrum of relationship between host and tenant churches is wide. Letting the space may be the only contact between the parties. At the other end of the spectrum the minister of the host church will meet from time to time with the ministers from tenant churches for fellowship and to pray together. In some cases the congregations will meet occasionally for a service of fellowship or a joint youth event. This is collaboration at its best because it allows mutual learning and mutual respect to develop.

In recent years Southwark diocese and black majority churches have been drawing closer in fellowship. A study day has drawn together Anglican and black majority church ministers to reflect on St John's gospel. Collaborative work has been done on a model tenancy agreement for church sharing, and further study encounters are planned. It is perhaps too early to try to evaluate the impact of these initiatives.

6 Where Do We Go From Here?

There are two new areas emerging which require attention—making liturgy more multicultural, and developing skills for leading predominantly BME parishes.

Multicultural Liturgy

In a small number of churches the music honours the heritage of BME members, such as the use of African drums, gospel music and occasionally hymns sung in a minority ethnic language as well as English. A few churches display non-white icons of Christ, the Madonna and, more rarely, a black saint like Martin de Porres of Brazil, and the African hero of the faith, Bernard Mizeki of Zimbabwe. These are the exception. For the great majority of churches the liturgy is very white Anglo-Saxon, and does not feel like all the people of God assembled in that place. This is an area where experimentation needs to be encouraged and resources developed. Creating multicultural liturgy is not part of the standard curriculum of theological colleges, and clergy may not feel confident in pioneering such an initiative on their own. Southwark diocese has begun to develop resources, and has published the booklet *Promised Land* which is a practical introduction to the subject.[19] John Danso's *Join In* provides useful ideas and a DVD resource on the subject.[20]

Clergy may not feel confident in pioneering multicultural liturgy

Some of the pressure for change is coming from BME members themselves. There is demand for thanksgiving services from members of African communities, to thank God for the many blessings he gives to his people (such as wedding anniversaries, recovery from illness, success in exams). Ministers may offer the family a special service, but this does not feel inclusive of everyone. A question to be wrestled with is how to integrate these events into Communion or all-age services? In the Caribbean community there is an emerging need for watchnight services on New Year's Eve, mirroring a tradition from the Caribbean. (Watchnight has an historic association with the slave trade. On 1 January enslaved Africans would be transferred from their plantations in settlement of debts by owners. On the previous night—New Year's Eve—slaves would gather for a service before any separations took place.) By its nature this would have to be an occasional service. These developments represent felt needs within congregations and call for a response from the church.

Leadership

Finally we look at leadership training for a new situation. The skills for leadership of predominantly BME congregations have come to the fore. The dynamics in the church can feel different from a church where the congregation is predominantly white. Here are some of the critical incidents clergy encounter. There may be low-level tension between different ethnic groups. Such tension may manifest itself in whispering campaigns against a black church warden, or a shove of one BME woman by another at the back of the communion queue. Tension may take the form of one black man refusing to take the chalice from an assistant of a different BME group. What if you are a white minister and your actions are evaluated against the prism of racism by some members? Have they got it right? Are they playing a race card? What impact does this have on you? Does it close down your options for intervention?

Authority in church in England is dispersed. At the parish level it is shared by the vicar, church wardens and the parochial church council. Such dispersal makes for a collaborative style of decision-making and working. Members of some ethnic groups have a different experience gained in their countries of heritage. Where the tradition is that a vicar is expected to make the decisions and solve the problem, deferring to the church council may appear to some members of a given community as a sign of weakness and indecision, and create an unfortunate dynamic between the vicar and the congregation. The challenge here is to recognize the issue of divergent concepts of authority, and to use skills of influencing and persuasion to change perceptions.

Improvisation When the Heat Is On

How does an incumbent respond to an expression of spirituality that is unfamiliar? God may be seen as intervening in the daily lives of members of the congregation—putting food on the table, protecting the children on the school bus, helping them through their exams, and bringing the rain. Some behaviours may be frowned on by white clergy, such as poor timekeeping, and lengthy tributes at funerals. Should these behaviours be challenged? Incidents such as these may be a cause for apprehension because they challenge the perceived way of doing things in Britain. They may be a cause of personal stress for the minister. There will be a need to ask questions and gather data in order to make sense of what is going on. Some degree of improvisation by the vicar may be required by way of response rather than a knee-jerk judgmental response.

There is the longer-term issue of whether the familiar model of church is appropriate. These cultural expressions butt up against the traditional model. Members might bring very different expectations about the role of the priest.

On the one hand the priest might be seen as ministering to the whole community; on the other he/she might be seen as the family's personal chaplain. Such expectations have to be recognized, understood and managed. There is room for and need for some retuning of the vision of church. What should the vision be? What are our values? As we encounter cultural practices of a pre-Christian nature, for example at funerals, how do we avoid becoming syncretistic?

It has been observed by some clergy that white people are now often coming to church for baptisms, marriages and funerals. Church is seen to offer commodities for which they are prepared to pay. The sense of church as a worshipping community has all but disappeared among some groups.

Where do people sit in church? Do the ethnic groups mix at the post-service event—tea, coffee? A visible indicator of how a church functions as a cohesive community is friendships across ethnic groups.

It becomes difficult to hold all this together by seeking to impose a particular set of cultural values. Yet with diverse values ministry can be scary. Some flexibility, willingness to go with the flow, capacity to learn on the hoof, and ability to 'tune the bandwidth' as you face scary situations seems like a good starting point. Leadership in such situations calls for some different skills from those normally applied to a culturally homogenous organization. There has to be a good deal of adapting to new situations and appropriate training in adaptive leadership styles.[21]

There are five factors that have been critical to the effectiveness of this programme of work. Let us examine each in turn.

Episcopally Led
The programme was led by the diocesan bishop from the start. He chaired and continues to chair the Minority Ethnic Anglican Concerns Committee (MEACC) which is charged with the responsibility to make it happen. Because the bishop gives visible leadership, office holders and staff take it seriously. The diocesan bishop also chairs a number of bodies which provide opportunities for him to reinforce the message of inclusiveness—Bishop's Council, Diocesan Synod to whom MEACC reports on a regular basis, and Bishop's Staff. Bishop's Council meets four times a year and each meeting receives the minutes of MEACC and can, if it wishes, raise any points with the staff officer who attends.

Rooted in Reality
Programmes which deal with race can be controversial and can be met with grudging acceptance or, at worst, resistance. From quite early on this programme sought to meet the needs of clergy and staff as they interfaced with

race. For example, the training programmes were based on needs analyses which focused on critical incidents in relationships between white and BME people, so clergy could see how the training would help them deliver a more effective ministry. For example, when clergy said it would be helpful to learn more about the cultures of BME people, on careful probing it turned out that cultural aspects of the occasional offices of baptisms, weddings and funerals were causing them difficulty. What is the significance of naming ceremonies? What are the cultural rituals around death and funerals? So the course was designed to include cross-cultural ministry.

Another example was the often-repeated observation that it was hard to get BME members to move beyond worship and participate in all aspects of church life. This led us to examining directly the processes for empowering minorities.

Targeted Key Areas

Key initiatives were directed where the need was greatest. It was important to tackle the BME deficits in the ordained and accredited ministries, hence the programme of vocations roadshows in churches with significant numbers of BME worshippers. Ideally there would be road shows in all 300 churches but these are resource-intensive so priority was given to churches with large BME membership.

Broad-based Collaboration

This work has to involve everyone. It cannot be done by the race experts. So MEACC staff worked closely with the ministry and training staff, the Diocesan Liturgical Committee, archdeacons and others to facilitate delivery of particular pieces of work.

Involving All Church Communities

The programme had to reach everyone, even if not everyone was actively engaged. Every opportunity was used to raise general levels of awareness of racial and cultural issues. MEACC's work was regularly reported in the diocesan newspaper, *The Bridge*. Racial Justice Sunday is marked every year on the second Sunday of September. The pack prepared for this is circulated free of charge to every parish, sometimes with a letter from Bishop Tom Butler encouraging clergy to celebrate the occasion. Key reports, for example on the 2007 ethnic survey, are circulated to all parishes for them to consider how the issues might relate to them and how they might respond. Even churches with no BME members have been included because they have a teaching role to perform for white members who, in work and other spheres, will come into contact with ethnic difference. The church's teaching in these matters may provide insights which enable its members to be more open and engaging with different others.

7 Conclusion

We cannot afford *not* to work hard at integrating minorities in the life and witness of the church. The BME presence of 17% overall of church membership far exceeds its representation in society at large, and it is a growing phenomenon. This booklet has tried to share some of the experience of one diocese in the Church of England which is committed to including and fully engaging members of diverse ethnic groups in all aspects of the life and witness of the church. White church membership is declining in Southwark diocese, and BME membership is growing rapidly. We cannot ignore this fact. Such growth is indeed a blessing.

> **We cannot afford not to work hard at integrating minorities**

The programme of work and approach described above has been fruitful in Southwark diocese. It has benefited in significant measure from being episcopally-led. Others may find some of the experience helpful to them. It may be difficult to replicate all of it in your individual local circumstances. For example, this model will not transfer to a church which is conciliar in governance. In such a situation, with more dispersed and consensual leadership, it will be necessary for the drive to come from the key ministers who influence the local church congregation. The elders, local clergy and the church councils become really critical to the success of such an initiative. They are the agencies which can mould opinion and influence members towards a common mind.

Other dioceses and denominations will have their own experiences in creating the multiethnic, multicultural church. It is hoped that some of what has worked in Southwark can be a basis for similar action in your church or area as together we strive in our time to breathe new life into the vision of the church at Antioch. This work is not finished, and there can be no guarantee that it will ever be completed, but a positive beginning has been made and the first fruits are coming through. We travel in faith on a journey in which we are God's agents. He is working his purpose out through us as we make his work our own, and in the fullness of time he will deliver the transformation we are striving for.

Notes

1   P Brierley, *Pulling Out of the Nosedive—A Contemporary Picture of Churchgoing* (London: Christian Research, 2006).

2   White and BME representation in English churches (English Church Attendance Survey, 2005).

Denomination	White	BME	Total	BME%
Anglican	767000	104000	871000	12
Baptist	224000	31000	255000	12
Roman Catholic	738000	155000	893000	17
Methodist	270000	19000	289000	7
Pentecostal	157000	131000	288000	45
United Reformed Church	65000	5000	70000	7
Others	420000	81000	501000	16
TOTAL	**2641000**	**526000**	**3166000**	**17**

3   T Cantle, *Community Cohesion—A New Framework for Race and Diversity* (Basingstoke: Palgrave Macmillan, 2005) p 6.

4   B Schwarz (ed), *West Indian Intellectuals in Britain* (Manchester University Press, 2003).

5   G Gordon-Carter, *An Amazing Journey—The Church of England's Response to Institutional Racism* (London: Church House Publishing, 2003). M Barton, *Rejection, Resistance and Resurrection—Speaking Out on Racism in the Church* (London: Darton, Longman and Todd, 2005).

6   Sir William MacPherson of Cluny, *The Stephen Lawrence Inquiry—Report of an Inquiry*, CM 4262-I, February 1999.

7   A le Grys, *Preaching to the Nations—Origins of Mission in the Early Christian Church* (London: SPCK 1998).

8   R Martin, *Ephesians, Colossians and Philemon* (Atlanta: John Knox Press, 1991).

9   J R W Stott, *God's New Society—the Message of Ephesians* (Nottingham: Inter-Varsity Press, 1979) chapters four and seven.

10   This sense of club takes on even greater significance as the Fresh Expressions initiative goes forward, and new church plants are grown around social networks. These are necessarily formed of like-minded people, and therefore more likely to be homogenous groups.

11   S Burgess and D Wilson, *Ethnic Segregation in England's Schools*, CMPO Working Paper 03/086, CMPO (University of Bristol, August 2003). ICoCo, *Building Community Cohesion in Britain*, Institute of Community Cohesion, February 2009.

12   M O Emerson with R M Woo, *People of the Dream—Multiracial Congregations in the United States* (Princeton, NJ: Princeton University Press, 2006).

13 J Sacks, *The Dignity of Difference* (London: Continuum, 2002).

14 See for example the General Synod report GS Misc 833, 'Church of England Clergy Diversity Audit 2005,' para 3.28, which records 23% of BME clergy as born in the UK, 57% born outside the UK and 20% not responding to the question about country of birth.

15 Archbishop of Canterbury's Commission on Urban Priority Areas, *Faith in the City—a Call to Action by Church and Nation* (London: Church House Publishing, 1985).

16 Diocese of Southwark, *Report of an Independent Inquiry into Institutional Racism Within the Structures of the Diocese of Southwark* (2000).

17 M Deymaz, *Building a Healthy Multiethnic Church* (Hoboken, NJ: Jossey-Bass, 2007). M O Emerson with R M Woo, *People of the Dream—Multiracial Congregations in the United States* (Princeton, NJ: Princeton University Press, 2006).

18 Diocese of Southwark, *Baptisms, Weddings and Funerals* (2006).

19 Diocese of Southwark, *Promised Land—Creating a Space for Diversity to Thrive* (2006).

20 J Danso, *Join In—Breaking Tradition, Embracing Culture: Styles of Multicultural Worship* (Ely: Melrose Books, 2009).

21 R Heifetz, *Leadership Without Easy Answers* (Cambridge, MA: Belknap Press, 1996). R Heifetz and Marty Linsky, *Leadership on the Line* (Boston, MA: Harvard Business School Press, 2002).